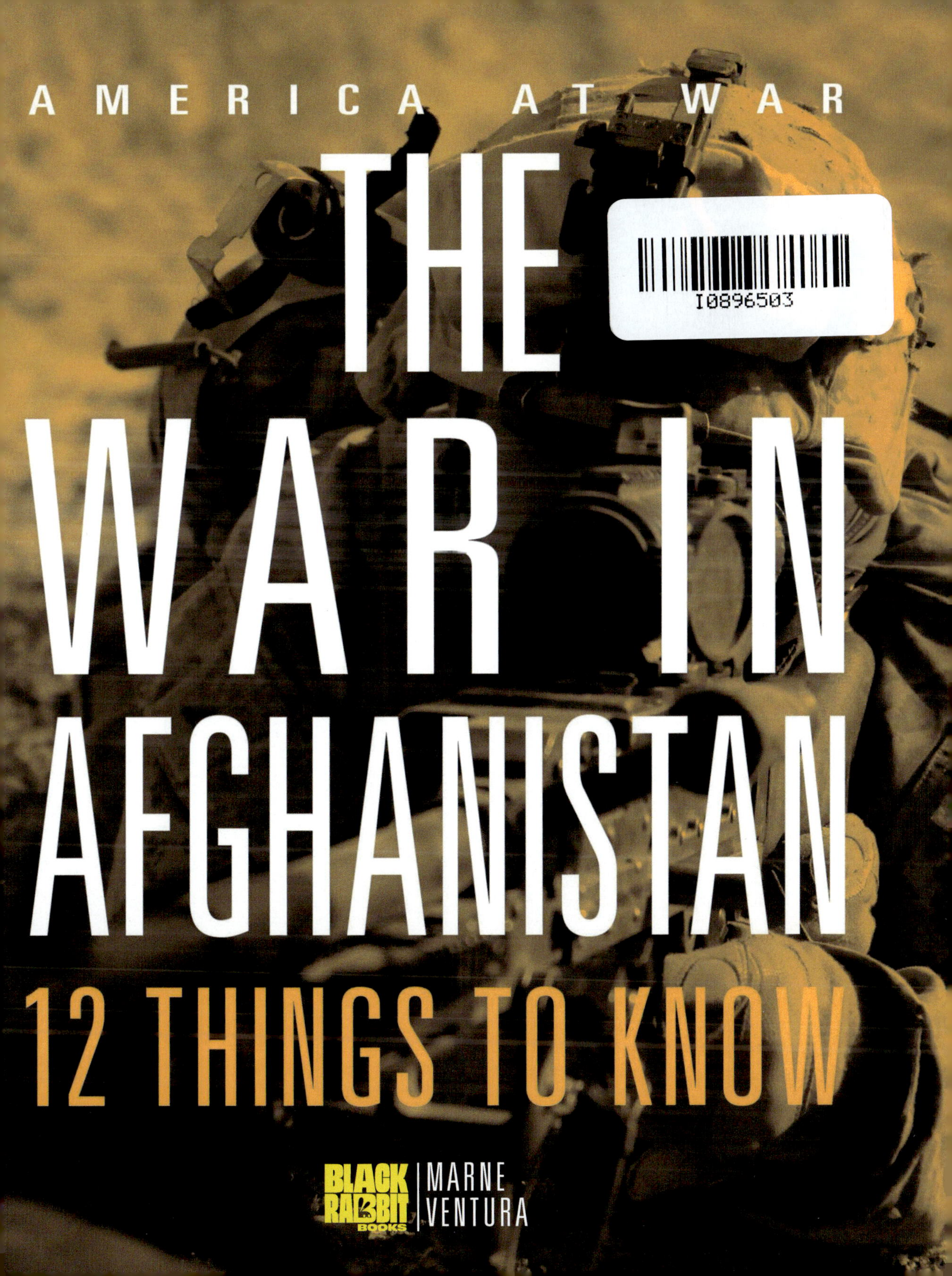

AMERICA AT WAR

THE WAR IN AFGHANISTAN

12 THINGS TO KNOW

BLACK RABBIT BOOKS

MARNE VENTURA

Table of Contents

252,000 Afghanistan's size, in square miles (652,677 square kilometers).

The country is west of Iran and east of Pakistan. • Most of the land is tall snowy mountains or dry deserts. • Many Afghans grow crops and raise animals in the valleys between mountains.

The Taliban Rises *from Chaos*

1

People have fought to control Afghanistan since ancient times. The country separates the Middle East and Asia. Its location is important for trade. One war began in 1978. A **communist** government took control of the country. People in the eastern part of the country fought it. By 1979, the country was in a civil war.

To the north was the Soviet Union. It was a communist nation. It joined the war to help the Afghan government. The United States helped the **rebels**. A wealthy Saudi man sent money to help the rebels too. His name was Osama bin Laden.

Bin Laden went to Afghanistan. He fought and trained other fighters. In 1989, both the Soviets and bin Laden left. This didn't stop the fighting, though. New governments were formed. They fell. Civil war spread through the country.

In 1994, a group called the Taliban was formed. In two years, they controlled the whole country. The Taliban promised peace. They followed a strict form of **Islam**. They banned music and movies. Women could not go to school or work. Groups against the Taliban gathered. They formed the Northern Alliance.

AL-QAEDA Osama bin Laden started a group called al-Qaeda. Its goal was to attack anyone against Islam. Islam is the **Muslim** religion. Bin Laden saw America as an enemy. He was forced out of Saudi Arabia for his beliefs. The Taliban supported him. He returned to Afghanistan in 1996.

Osama bin Laden founded al-Qadea in 1988.

9/11 Attacks Lead *to War*

2

September 11, 2001, began with calm skies over New York City. That changed at 8:46 a.m. A plane crashed into the North Tower of the World Trade Center. People thought it was an accident. But then, a second plane hit the South Tower. It was no accident after all.

About 34 minutes later, another plane crashed into the Pentagon. That is in Arlington, Virginia. It is the headquarters of the US military. A fourth plane was heading to Washington, DC. It might have hit the White House or the Capitol. Instead, the passengers stopped the attack. The plane crashed in a field in Pennsylvania. Everyone onboard died.

Americans were shocked by the attacks. People around the world sent their sympathy. Citizens from more than 80 countries had lost their lives. The day would be forever known as 9/11.

The South Tower was hit 17 minutes after the North Tower.

2,996 Number of people who died in the 9/11 attacks.

The Twin Towers were the tallest buildings in New York City. • Many more people were injured. • Many rescue workers lost their lives trying to save people.

Terrorists from al-Qaeda were responsible. President George W. Bush said the attacks were acts of war. He told the Taliban to hand over bin Laden. The Taliban refused. The US government got ready for war.

Bush said the war was not against Islam. It was against terrorism. The United States asked other countries for help. Some countries offered ways into Afghanistan. Others sent troops. The **allies** formed a **coalition**. Bush warned the Taliban: Time was running out.

THINK ABOUT IT

After 9/11, many countries stepped forward. They agreed to help the United States with the war on terrorism. Why?

9/11 Memorial in Manhattan, NY

Operation Enduring Freedom *Begins*

3

It was the night of October 7, 2001. A huge ship floated in the Arabian Sea. A plane took off from its deck. The bomber was headed for Afghanistan. **Operation** Enduring Freedom was about to begin.

Other bombers joined in. They were US and British planes. Some came from as far away as Missouri. The 44-hour flight was the longest bombing mission ever.

The mission had two goals. The first was to destroy al-Qaeda. The second was to bring down the Taliban. The Taliban had protected bin Laden even after 9/11. The planes bombed al-Qaeda camps. They struck the Taliban's military sites. Training camps were also targets.

The United States and its allies did not want to take over Afghanistan. They wanted the people to support

the war. So they tried to limit **civilian** deaths. They gave aid to people caught in the fighting. And they helped the Northern Alliance. Local fighters were armed. Working together, they could defeat the Taliban.

THINK ABOUT IT

The Taliban banned many things. How would your life be different without games, music, and movies? Would you risk being punished to have those things?

Northern Alliance fighters prepare for battle with the Taliban.

34,400 Number of **aid** packets dropped the first night of Operation Enduring Freedom.

The coalition dropped leaflets to explain that the attacks were for the Taliban. • US planes also dropped radios. • These were preset to a station that explained the purpose of the war.

An American soldier comforts an Afghan child.

4 Kandahar Falls, Bringing Down *the Taliban*

The Northern Alliance swept across Afghanistan. They did not have huge numbers. But now they had help. The United States and their allies sent supplies. When the Taliban fought back, US planes bombed them.

Alliance troops moved to Kabul. That was the capital city. The Afghan people welcomed them. The Taliban tried to keep their hold in the city. But air strikes had hurt their numbers. Ground and air forces drove them back. They were forced to flee.

On November 13, 2001, the Northern Alliance took over Kabul. It had not been planned. Many countries told them to ignore Kabul. But the Alliance felt that the city needed help. The people were happy to be free from the Taliban. Music played in the streets for the first time in years.

Planes like the Boeing B-52 were used to drop bombs on the Taliban.

5 Number of years the Taliban ruled Afghanistan.

On November 14, the United Nations (UN) gave its full support to the Afghan people. • The UN had a central role in setting up a new government. • Its member states sent forces to help Afghanistan.

The Taliban still held Kandahar. This is a big city in the south. The United States and allies pressed forward. They were ready for a fight. The city fell quickly. It was out of Taliban control on December 7. Two days later, Zabul Province was also free. That was the Taliban's last hold in Afghanistan. Their rule had finally ended.

UNITED NATIONS The United Nations (UN) is made up of 193 countries. It works to maintain worldwide peace and security. It tries to keep nations friendly. It also works to improve living conditions for people.

Bonn Agreement Shows a Way *Forward*

5

The Taliban was gone. Afghanistan needed new leaders. Different **ethnic** groups fought. They did not agree about the country's future.

The United Nations (UN) chose a **neutral** place for them to meet. On November 27, 2001, a meeting was held in Bonn, Germany. More than two dozen leaders came. They represented four different Afghan groups. Some groups did not trust the others. There was a bad history between them. There was arguing. But they all knew decisions had to be made.

On December 5, they signed an agreement. Hamid Karzai was chosen to lead a temporary government. It would start on December 22. Karzai was a Pashtun. Most people in the country were Pushtun. It would be easier to accept another Pushtun as a leader.

Hamid Karzai

The Afghans wanted to protect their country. They needed to build an army. They needed a police force. Those could not be formed overnight. It would take time. Until then, they asked the United Nations to help. UN troopers would keep the peace. They were called the International Security Assistance Force (ISAF).

2 Number of women who were given roles in the new government.

Women had been shut out of public life under the Taliban. • The new government asked for help from other nations to rebuild Afghanistan. • It also asked the UN to help set up an election.

US troops rappel out of a helicopter to drop to the ground in Afghanistan.

NATO The United States is part of the North Atlantic Treaty Organization (NATO). Twenty-eight countries belong to NATO. The UN and NATO work together. After 9/11, NATO agreed to support the war against the Taliban. Starting on August 11, 2003, NATO led the ISAF. They helped rebuild Afghanistan.

Battle of Tora Bora Misses *bin Laden*

6

The Taliban and al-Qaeda were on the run. Many members fled to Tora Bora. This was in the eastern part of the country. It was part of a mountain range and close to Pakistan. A base had been built there during the Soviet invasion. It was 6 square miles (9.7 square km). And bin Laden knew the caves well. He had fought there. Later, he built a home nearby.

Al-Qaeda used the caves to train. They stored weapons inside. The caves offered good shelter. They were good protection from bombs.

The United States did not want bin Laden to get away. But they also did not want to lead the attack. They wanted Afghans to be in charge. The Northern Alliance made plans to storm the caves. The mission was to take full control.

First, cave entrances were bombed from the air. The explosions caused landslides. Some caves were buried. Weapons and vehicles were lost. Next, Afghans led the ground assault. This was very dangerous. Members of al-Qaeda fought to the death.

The mission was a partial success. The Alliance took control of the caves. But many Taliban and al-Qaeda members escaped. That included bin Laden.

NEIGHBORING COUNTRIES Afghanistan and Pakistan are neighbors. Pakistan was one of the only countries that accepted the Taliban as leaders. Later, Pakistan agreed to help NATO. But the Taliban still had safe places in both countries. Pakistan's government did not have much control over the border. Many people in Pakistan had ties with the Taliban.

An Afghan fighter pops up from his tank to watch a US warplane bombing Tora Bora.

Allied soldiers search caves in Tora Bora for Taliban members.

9 Distance in miles (14 km) to Pakistan from Tora Bora.

The battle of Tora Bora lasted from December 3 to 17, 2001. • The United States sent B-52 air strikes to the area. • The allied forces included British, German, and US forces.

7 Operation Anaconda Squeezes *Taliban*

In 2002, it looked like the war might be near an end. But the new Afghan government faced an old danger. Members of al-Qaeda and the Taliban had survived attacks and air strikes. Some had hidden in the mountains of southeastern Afghanistan. Others were in Pakistan. These fighters began to gather again. They chose Shah-e-Kot Valley. It was near Tora Bora. The coalition moved to stop them.

The mission was called Operation Anaconda. It would be the largest combat operation during the war. For the first time, US forces were a big part of the ground fight. **Special operations** troops from across Europe and North America gathered. They were joined by Afghan allies.

The valley covered around 60 square miles (155 square km). Three villages were in the valley. Most villagers had

American soldiers find a dead Taliban fighter in March 2002.

fled. The plan was to secure the valley and the mountain passes. This would block enemies trying to flee.

The attack began on March 2. It was still dark out. Snow scattered the ground. The valley was believed to be mostly empty. But al-Qaeda fighters had hidden themselves from drones. Some troops found themselves under heavy fire. Bad weather slowed others down as they fought toward their targets.

The fierce battle lasted for days. In the end, US troops won. The coalition controlled the valley by March 12. Fighting ended a week later. The allies did not agree about the results. The United States claimed only a few men escaped. Al-Qaeda claimed hundreds got out alive.

7 Number of countries involved in combat in Operation Anaconda.

There were about 2,000 coalition troops. • The battle ended as an American win. • Eight US soldiers were killed. Fifty were wounded.

Taliban Fights Back *with IEDs*

8

The new Afghan government held its first election on October 9, 2004. The people chose Hamid Karzai for president. Their lives were getting better. Roads and buildings had been rebuilt. Children were receiving health care. Girls were going back to school. But the country was still not stable. Not everyone liked the new government. Some were angry. Coalition strikes on the Taliban had killed people they knew. Some Afghan officials were dishonest. Many people were poor.

Improvised explosive device (IED)

The Taliban wanted to end the new government. Their fighters attacked military bases with bombs and rockets. They attacked Afghan civilians and troops. They targeted aid and government workers. In parts of Afghanistan, they moved around freely. Other Taliban and al-Qaeda fighters stayed in Pakistan. They crossed the border to attack. Then they went back to Pakistan.

50 Approximate number of Taliban attacks per month for most of 2005.

Taliban fighters used IEDs to attack the coalition. • Most IEDs are set off by a trip wire or pressure plate. Others need a remote control. • Some IEDs use timers.

SOLDIERS AID AFGHANS During its rule, the Taliban had kept girls out of school. Coalition soldiers handed out food, clothes, and school supplies in 2006. They helped build schools. One was a school for girls. Anti-government fighters still opposed girls' schools. They attacked students and teachers. But locals were excited to learn again.

Taliban fighters used homemade bombs called **IEDs**. The IEDs were set next to roads or paths. They were left in houses soldiers might search. For safety, coalition soldiers drove armored trucks. The armor protected them from a blast. But civilians were not protected. They were often hurt by IEDs.

Military troops drive an armed humvee that protects them from IEDs.

Drones Reduce Risks *to Soldiers*

9

Armed drones were heavily used in Afghanistan. They had flown ever since the first night of Operation Enduring Freedom. A drone is controlled remotely by someone. Drones can be used to spy on people and targets. No pilot is injured if the drone is shot down.

The United States has used drones in several wars. Unpiloted planes carried bombs in World War II (1939–45). Drones took photos during the Vietnam War (1955–75). A drone even watched bin Laden in 2000. But that drone had no weapons. And soldiers couldn't reach him in time. After 9/11, drones were armed.

Many drones are controlled using a remote and a tablet.

Modern drones have video cameras. They serve as scouts. They help soldiers prepare for military operations. They were used in Operation Anaconda. Drones spied on enemy fighters in Afghanistan. They carried rifles and even missiles.

In 2008, even more drones were used. They were sent to Pakistan. They found where the Taliban was hiding. Drones could fly over remote areas, unseen. Their cameras spied on the Taliban. Weapons were used to take enemies down.

Hexacopter drone

12,000 Speed in miles (19,312 km) per hour that a military drone can reach.

Drones can have real-time video streaming. • A drone is an unmanned aerial vehicle (UAV). • Drones help the military save lives. They keep pilots safe on the ground.

Military drones often look like small planes with cameras and weapons.

THINK ABOUT IT Some people do not agree with the military using drones. Why do you think that is? What is your opinion?

Troops Surge to Subdue *Taliban*

10

In 2003, the Iraq War began. Many US troops were sent to Iraq. The Taliban was able to gain much of their power back in Afghanistan.

In 2009, President Barack Obama took office. He had to decide what to do. He could not just leave the Taliban to control Afghanistan again. He approved a plan to send thousands of new troops there. The troops could push back the Taliban. They would win back old land. Obama hoped it would be fast. He wanted to bring the new troops home in less than two years.

The first task was to take the city of Marja. At the time, Marja was the Taliban's headquarters. The area supported the Taliban with money from the production of illegal drugs. The United States warned the Taliban to leave

President Barack Obama

30,000 Number of US troops sent to fight.

President Obama sent soldiers from all military branches. • The US military worked to train Afghan forces. • When the US troops left in 2012, Afghans took over.

US soldiers patrol areas in Afghanistan.

the area. It wanted to limit fighting to reduce civilian deaths. Marines flew into Marja on February 13, 2010. They attacked from all directions. IEDs were everywhere. After a short fight, the Taliban gave up.

US troops continued to fight throughout the south. They found local Afghans who wanted to help. They aided with construction and government. The US troops left in September 2012. Afghan forces stayed behind. Their job was to keep the peace. But some Afghans worried their own troops could not hold things together. They did not have enough **discipline** or fire power.

An Afghan terrorist surrenders.

US Combat Mission *Ends*

11

War is expensive. Operation Enduring Freedom was no exception. Many lives were lost. Almost 10,000 civilians were killed in 2014 alone. About 5,000 Afghan troops died. Journalists and **humanitarian** workers lost their lives too. Although the fighting continued, the United States was tired of war. Bin Laden, a main target of the war, had been killed in Pakistan on May 2, 2011. Afghanistan now had more than 350,000 of its own troops. It was time for US troops to leave.

On December 28, 2014, ISAF held a service at its headquarters in Kabul. People from many countries came. The green and white ISAF flag flying over the headquarters was lowered. A general rolled it up. The war in Afghanistan was officially over. The Afghan military now took the lead. President Obama was not at the event, but he spoke about it. He said the war had **disrupted** terrorism and helped Afghans.

But the world did not abandon Afghanistan completely. The general who folded the ISAF flag brought out a new one. This flag represented Operation Resolute Support. It was a new international mission led by NATO. The United States also began Operation Freedom's Sentinel on January 1, 2015. As part of this operation, nearly 10,000 US troops stayed behind. The focus of the two new missions would be training and supporting Afghan forces.

$2.3 trillion Approximate cost of the war, from 2001 to 2022.

It is one of the most expensive wars in US history.
• Most of the war was paid on credit. • In total, there were around 243,000 casualties of the war.

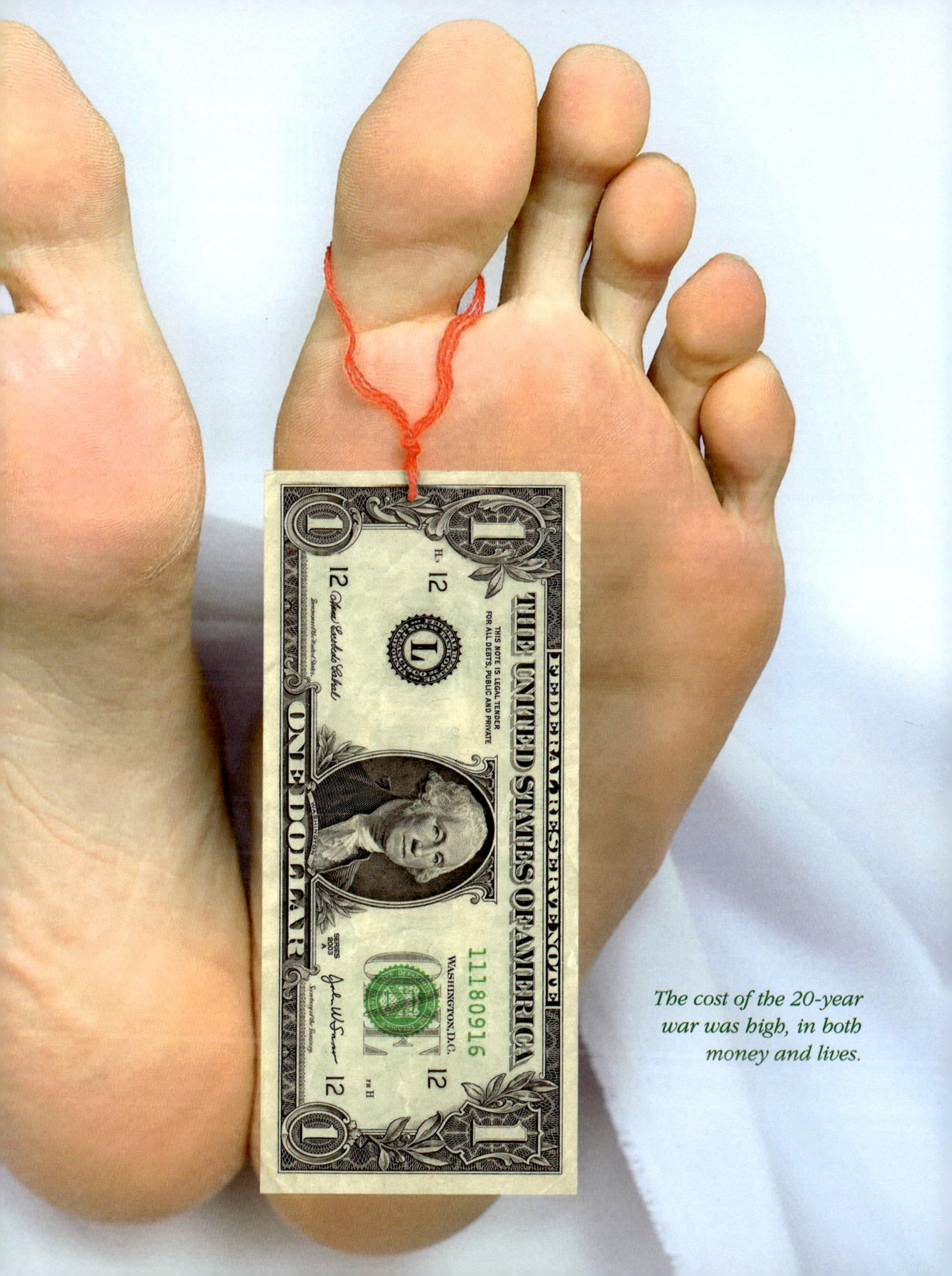

The cost of the 20-year war was high, in both money and lives.

United States Withdraws *Troops*

12

President Obama planned to bring all US troops home by the end of 2016. But on October 15, 2015, he made an announcement. The Taliban and al-Qaeda were no longer the only threats in the area. Thousands of US troops would stay in Afghanistan through 2017. They might even have to stay longer.

The US also was concerned about a new terrorist group. It was called the Islamic State of Iraq and Syria (ISIS). It followed a harsh form of Islam. ISIS was taking over parts of Syria and Iraq. US troops continued to train and support Afghan forces. They knew another hard fight was coming.

On February 29, 2020, the US and the Taliban signed a peace agreement. US troops would pull out of Afghanistan over 14 months. The Taliban would take part in peace talks with the Afghan government. The Taliban would stop al-Qaeda and ISIS from fighting. The US began to pull out troops. By January 2021, just 3,500 of the 13,000 troops remained.

In 2021, President Joe Biden declared the United States would bring the rest of the troops home. On August 6, the Taliban re-took control of their first city. Afghan forces were unable to stop them. By August 31, 2021, the Afghan government collapsed. The Taliban took control of the country again.

Transport helicopters move supplies to ground troops.

The last American troops left Afghanistan in August 2021.

69 Percent of Americans who felt the United States had failed in Afghanistan.

The Taliban did not obey the peace agreement. • The US withdrawal caused chaos. • Tens of thousands of Afghans rushed to the Kabul airport. They were trying to escape the Taliban.

12 Key Dates

September 11, 2001
Al-Qaeda attacks the United States with planes, hitting the World Trade Center and the Pentagon.

October 7, 2001
Operation Enduring Freedom begins with bombs dropped across Afghanistan.

November 13, 2001
The Northern Alliance enters Kabul, the capital of Afghanistan.

December 9, 2001
The Taliban loses control of Afghanistan.

March 2, 2002
Operation Anaconda attacks Taliban forces gathering in a valley.

October 9, 2004
Afghanistan holds its first elections and Hamid Karzai keeps the presidency.

September 11, 2001

November 13, 2001

October 9, 2004

February 13, 2010
Extra troops from the surge attack Marja, a Taliban stronghold.

May 2, 2011
US troops kill Osama bin Laden in Pakistan.

December 28, 2014
The war officially ends with a ceremony in Kabul.

January 1, 2015
The United States begins Operation Freedom's Sentinel to support Afghan forces.

August 21, 2017
US troops are sent to help Afghan forces.

February 29, 2020
US and Taliban agree on framework for US withdrawal.

May 2, 2011

February 13, 2010

Glossary

ally
A country that supports and helps another country in a war.

aid
Help or assistance that is given to someone in need.

civilian
A person not in the armed services.

coalition
A group of allies working for a common goal.

communist
To be a part of a system of government in which all property is controlled by the government.

discipline
Control that is gained by requiring that rules or order be obeyed and punishing bad behavior.

disrupt
To interrupt the progress or activity of something.

ethnic
Of or relating to races or large groups of people who have the same customs, religion, and origin.

humanitarian
Working to improve society and people's lives.

IED
Stands for improvised explosive device; a simple bomb made and used by unofficial or unauthorized forces.

Islam
A religion that believes there is only one God and follows the teachings of Muhammad, called the Prophet of Allah.

Muslim
A follower of Islam.

neutral
Not connected with either side involved in a war.

operation
A set of planned actions for a particular purpose.

special operations
Military activities that use small, highly trained units that require unusual techniques and modes of service.

rebel
A person who opposes or fights against a government.

terrorist
Someone who uses violence to scare people, often to achieve a political goal.

For More Information

Books

Billings, Tanner. *Cyber Tech in Warfare*. Buffalo, NY: Cavendish Square Publishing, 2023.

Marlin, Charles. *Drones*. Mendota Heights: Apex Editions, 2025.

Winter, Max. *Afghanistan War*. Parker: The Child's World, 2024.

Websites

Afghanistan Country Profile
www.bbc.com/news/world-south-asia-12011352

Timeline: The U.S. War in Afghanistan
www.cfr.org/timeline/us-war-afghanistan

US History: War in Afghanistan
www.ducksters.com/history/us_1900s/war_in_afghanistan.php

About the Author

Marne Ventura is a children's book author and a former elementary school teacher. She holds a master's degree in education with an emphasis in reading and language development from the University of California.

Index

TOP RANK is published by Black Rabbit Books, P.O. Box 227, Mankato, MN, 56002. •

• Designed by Danny Nanos • Photographs © Alamy Stock Photo/Everett Collection, 23, Laperruque, 9, 44; Associated Press/DAVID GUTTENFELDER, 22, Jason Whitman, 24; Dreamstime/Abhishek Singh, 12, 16, 22, 44, 45, Alan Crosthwaite, 10, Arisha Singh, 19, Bumbleedee, 42, Fatih Kurtcan, 2, Markwaters, 17, 44, Mustapha Gunnouni, 16, Robert Sholl, 28-29, Zim235, 6; Getty Images/Getty Images, 7, RAHMATULLAH ALIZADAH, 37, Robert Nickelsberg, 25; Shutterstock/Actium, 42–43, AndriiKoval, 14, AustralianCamera, 4, Belinda Pretorius, 48, Carolina K. Smith MD, 45, charnsitr, 35, 45, Christopher Chambers, 15, De Visu, 18, Everett Collection, 27, Ezume Images, 16, Frank Wagner, 8, GoodAndy45, cover, 1, gowithstock, 10, grafvision, 36, Grindstone Media Group, 34, Ground Picture, 30, Irfan ali turi, 21, Jolygon, 46–47, Militarist, 27, Northfoto, 12, Oleg Yarko [site: Yarko.Tv], 2-3, 32–33, Samo Trebizan, 31, Valeriy Minin, 39, VanderWolf Images, 40, 41, Viacheslav Lopatin, 20, WOSUNAN, 5; Wikimedia Commons/MCSN Laura Hoover, 11, Staff Sgt. Dayton Mitchell, 13

Library of Congress Cataloging-in-Publication Data: Names: Ventura, Marne author | Title: The war in Afghanistan: 12 things to know / by Marne Ventura. | Description: Mankato, MN: Top Rank is an imprint of Black Rabbit Books, [2026] | Series: America at war | Includes bibliographical references and index. | Grades 4–6 | Ages 9–13 | Identifiers: LCCN 2024050099 | ISBN 9781644668245 (library binding) | ISBN 9781644668566 (paperback) | ISBN 9781644668887 (ebook) | Subjects: LCSH: Afghan War, 2001–2021—Miscellanea—Juvenile literature | Afghan War, 2001–2021—United States—Miscellanea—Juvenile literature | Classification: LCC DS371.412 .V46 2026 | DDC 958.104/7—dc23/eng/20241122 | LC record available at https://lccn.loc.gov/2024050099